Spotlight on™ Reasoning & Problem Solving
Making Predictions & Inferences

by Paul F. Johnson & Carolyn LoGiudice

Skills
- predicting
- inferencing
- reasoning

Ages
- 6 through 12

Grades
- 1 through 7

Evidence-Based Practice

According to the Clinical Guidelines of the Royal College of Speech & Language Therapists (www.rcslt.org/resources, 2005) and Speech-Language Guidelines for Schools with a Focus on Research-Based Practices (www.kansped.org/ksde/resources/speech-guide/pdf, 2005), the following therapy principles are supported:

- Oral language development, including semantic skills, has a direct bearing on literate language development.

- Difficulties with vocabulary can include understanding concepts, semantic relationships among words, and storage/retrieval of words.

- Children need good vocabulary skills in order to become independent learners.

- Children require strategic instruction to access the curriculum to the best of their abilities.

- Essential language skills that impact students' academic performance include the ability to verbalize semantic categories and specific features for words, compare/contrast skills, reading comprehension strategies, and problem-solving language skills.

The tasks in this book incorporate the above principles and are also based on expert professional practice.

LinguiSystems®

LinguiSystems, Inc.
3100 4th Avenue
East Moline IL 61244

FAX: 800-577-4555
Phone: 800-776-4332
E-mail: service@linguisystems.com
Web: linguisystems.com

Copyright © 2007 LinguiSystems, Inc.

All of our products are copyrighted to protect the fine work of our authors. You may only copy the student materials as needed for your own use. Any other reproduction or distribution of the pages in this book is prohibited, including copying the entire book to use as another primary source or "master" copy.

The enclosed CD is for your personal use and convenience. It is unlawful to copy this CD or store its content on a multi-user network.

Printed in the U.S.A.

ISBN 978-0-7606-0727-5

About the Authors

Paul F. Johnson, B.A., and **Carolyn LoGiudice**, M.S., CCC-SLP, are editors and writers for LinguiSystems. They have collaborated to develop several publications, including *Story Comprehension To Go*, *No-Glamour Sequencing Cards*, and *Spotlight on Reading & Listening Comprehension*. Paul and Carolyn share a special interest in boosting students' language, critical thinking, and academic skills.

In their spare time, Paul and Carolyn enjoy their families, music, gourmet cooking, and reading. Paul, a proud father of three children, also enjoys bicycling, playing music, and spending rare moments alone with his wife, Kenya. Carolyn is learning to craft greeting cards and spoil grandchildren.

Illustrations by Margaret Warner
Cover design by Jeff Taylor
Page layout by Christine Buysse
Editing by Kelly Malone

Table of Contents

Introduction 4

Pretest/Posttest 6

Detecting Absurdities 7

Getting Information from Pictures 13

Predicting with Pictures 16

Predicting from Book Covers 18

Predicting with Choices 20

Predicting 24

Identifying Causes 26

Making Inferences with Pictures 30

Making Inferences Without Pictures 35

Answer Key 40

Introduction

Reasoning and problem solving are not simply life skills, they are *quality of life* skills. Throughout our lives, the abilities to reason and solve problems are the difference between succeeding or failing in academic pursuits, making good and bad everyday decisions, and improving or destroying social relationships.

The world assumes we come to it with well-developed reasoning and problem-solving skills, but that is not always the case. Because of language delays and other factors, many students lack basic skills to achieve positive outcomes in academic and everyday living situations.

The goal of *Spotlight on Reasoning & Problem Solving* is to build skills, step-by-step, using a focused instructional approach. The situations students will use for practice in these books are ones many of them have faced or will face throughout their lives. We support the approach that Richard Paul suggests in his landmark 1990 book, *Critical Thinking*:

> ". . . because we can form new ideas, beliefs, and patterns of thought only through the scaffolding of our previously formed thought, it is essential that we learn to think critically in environments in which a variety of competing ideas are taken seriously." (page xv)

Before students can reach and approach the kind of proficiency Paul describes, they must fully understand and master the building blocks of reasoning and problem solving. *Spotlight on Reasoning & Problem Solving* presents six crucial areas for developing the language-based thinking skills that, when mastered, provide students with the tools to become better thinkers and problem solvers:

- Causes & Effects
- Comparing & Contrasting
- Facts & Opinions
- Making Predictions & Inferences
- Sequencing
- Solving Problems

Most students will benefit from working through each book from beginning to end. Even if a student's proficiency is beyond the initial activities presented, the feeling of success he experiences by mastering them will motivate him to approach the more challenging activities that follow with confidence.

Students need to predict, determine causes, and make logical inferences in their daily lives as well as in academic situations. The tasks in this book are designed to help students consider their own experiences as well as their increasing knowledge of others' thoughts and experiences in order to make logical inferences. The beginning tasks ensure students are able to detect absurdities and to detect essential information from pictures. Next, students make predictions based on picture clues, including book cover information. Tasks then progress to making predictions without picture clues, first with a multiple-choice format and then without any answers provided. After practicing determining causes of events, students tackle making inferences with and without picture clues.

Introduction, continued

As you present these tasks, encourage your students to think about everything they know about each situation before they jump to conclusions. For multiple-choice formats, they should consider each choice carefully before selecting the best answer.

Here are some additional activities to develop students' skills in predicting and making inferences.

- To introduce inferences, demonstrate various ways of walking or sitting and ask your students to guess your mood along with a logical trigger for your mood (timid, adventurous, etc.). You can do the same thing by presenting snippets of people's voices or pictures of people in various contexts.

- Play Pantomime with your students, using stimuli of everyday activities or common emotional responses (brushing teeth, making a sandwich, feeling anxious about something, etc.). You can either have the whole group guess what a single performer is doing or divide the group into smaller teams. Notice whether individual students make logical guesses or off-the-wall guesses as well as whether they take adequate thinking time before making a guess.

- On the board or an overhead, make two columns headed "What We Know" and "What We Guess." Present pictures or short situations, including some from the tasks in this book, and have the group collectively add information to the appropriate columns to work toward a logical inference.

- Frequently ask your students, "Why are we doing/learning this?" to help them see the logical cause and effect of your instruction and their learning or enrichment.

- As often as possible when students make inferences, ask them, "How do you know that?" or "What clues make you think that?" Also model making good inferences orally by commenting on what you infer based on students' behavior or on information from a classroom lesson.

We hope you and your students enjoy working through these activities together, and we are certain that with your guidance, your students' reasoning and problem-solving skills will improve with each completed page.

Paul and Carolyn

Pretest/Posttest

1. What's silly about this? Bryce burned his tongue while drinking orange juice.

2. What's silly about this? Lewis liked to walk in the rain. He splashed in puddles along the way. Then he made his shadow imitate fun dance moves.

3. Why did Amanda frown when Ms. Carson passed out yesterday's test?

4. Mason had ketchup on his shirt and his pants after lunch. What had happened?

5. Tory turned the water on to take a bath. He made sure the water temperature was just right, but the tub wouldn't fill up. Why?

6. When we sat down at the restaurant, we knew three people had already eaten in the same booth. How did we know that?

7. Kelly told Dan a secret about her dad. Dan promised not to tell anyone, but two days later, Kelly's friends said, "We're sorry to hear about your dad." How did Kelly feel? Why?

Write three reasons a teacher might be absent from school.

8.

9.

10.

Detecting Absurdities ❶

→ Explain to your students that you will be doing some silly things. They should watch what you do and point out what is silly. Ask them to explain why it is silly and what you should do that makes more sense.

You will need these props:

- book
- pencil
- glasses or sunglasses
- paper
- crayon or marker
- pencil sharpener
- your country's flag
- potted plant
- watering can or container

1. Write your last name backwards on the board.
2. Erase a chalkboard or white board with a pencil eraser.
3. Cover your eyes (instead of your mouth) while you yawn widely.
4. Walk across the room backwards.
5. Take off your shoes and put them on the wrong feet.
6. Wear glasses or sunglasses on your leg.
7. Write on paper while you look up with your eyes closed.
8. Try to sharpen a crayon/marker in a pencil sharpener.
9. Face away from the flag and pledge allegiance.
10. Mouth directions for your students to do something. Do not make a sound.
11. Stack objects on your desk into a tower.
12. Close the window shades/blinds and turn off the lights.
13. Use made-up names as you greet a few students. Instead of a handshake, shake each student's elbow.
14. Water a plant without using any water in the watering container.
15. Write the incorrect date on the board.
16. Read a book upside down.

Detecting Absurdities ❷

→ Find five silly things in this picture. Then turn the page upside down to check the answers.

guitar in oven, stirring with a rake, eggs falling off the table, cook book upside down, chef is a bear

Detecting Absurdities ❸

→ Find at least six silly things in this picture. Then turn the page upside down to check the answers.

The legs of the teacher's pants are different lengths.
A turtle is on a leash in a classroom.
A boy is pouring cereal on his head.
A dog is in the classroom, licking milk like a cat.

A clown is sitting in a student's desk.
A camel is in the classroom.
A girl is reading a book while riding on the camel.

Spotlight on Reasoning & Problem Solving
Making Predictions & Inferences

Detecting Absurdities ❹

➜ Tell what is silly about each picture.

Detecting Absurdities 5

➜ Write what is silly about each picture.

1.

2.

Detecting Absurdities 6

→ Read each paragraph and check the best answer for each question.

1. I started to walk to school this morning. The sun was so bright, it hurt my eyes. I went back inside and found a flashlight. Then I could see better on my way to school.

    What is silly about that?
    ____ a. You don't walk to school in the morning.
    ____ b. You don't need a flashlight to see when the light is bright.
    ____ c. A flashlight is too heavy to carry to school.

2. My dad owns a horse stable. He has eight horses people can ride. Today all of our horses were out riding by 9:00. Another man came to ride a horse. Since we wouldn't have any more horses for a while, we let him ride our giraffe instead.

    What is silly about that?
    ____ a. People don't ride giraffes.
    ____ b. People don't ride horses.
    ____ c. Only children can ride giraffes.

3. We had a big storm yesterday. The river flooded many roads and homes. One bridge was closed, so people drove across the water. By tomorrow the roads should be okay.

    What is silly about that?
    ____ a. A river can't flood roads or homes.
    ____ b. You can't drive a car on water.
    ____ c. You can't close a bridge.

4. Our dog is really smart! He does lots of tricks and he never chews on anything but his special bone. He reads faster than I can, and he sleeps in my bedroom.

    What is silly about that?
    ____ a. A dog can't read.
    ____ b. A dog wouldn't sleep in a bedroom.
    ____ c. Dogs don't chew on bones.

Spotlight on Reasoning & Problem Solving
Making Predictions & Inferences

Getting Information from Pictures ❶

→ Look at each picture carefully. Then check the best answer to the question.

1.

   What is this girl doing?

   ____ a. She is taking baked cookies out of the oven.

   ____ b. She is putting cookies into the oven to bake.

   ____ c. She is baking cookies in a microwave oven.

2.

   What is this person doing?

   ____ a. He is looking for something good to eat.

   ____ b. He is packing his backpack.

   ____ c. He is bagging groceries in a grocery store.

Getting Information from Pictures ❷

➜ Look at each picture carefully. Then check the best answer to the question.

1. Look at the girl in the middle of this picture. What is she doing?

____ a. She is wrapping a present.

____ b. She is singing a song.

____ c. She has just opened a birthday present.

2. What are these children making for their art project?

____ a. book covers

____ b. ladybugs

____ c. flowers

Spotlight on Reasoning & Problem Solving
Making Predictions & Inferences

Getting Information from Pictures ❸

→ Look at each picture carefully. Then write what is missing from each picture.

1
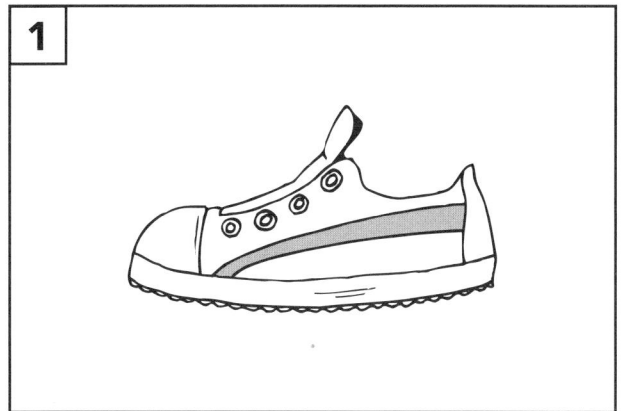

_____

2

_____

3

_____

4

_____

5

_____

6

_____

Predicting with Pictures ❶

→ Look at each picture carefully. Then check the best answer to the question.

1. Molly is carrying a bag of dog food. What will she do next?

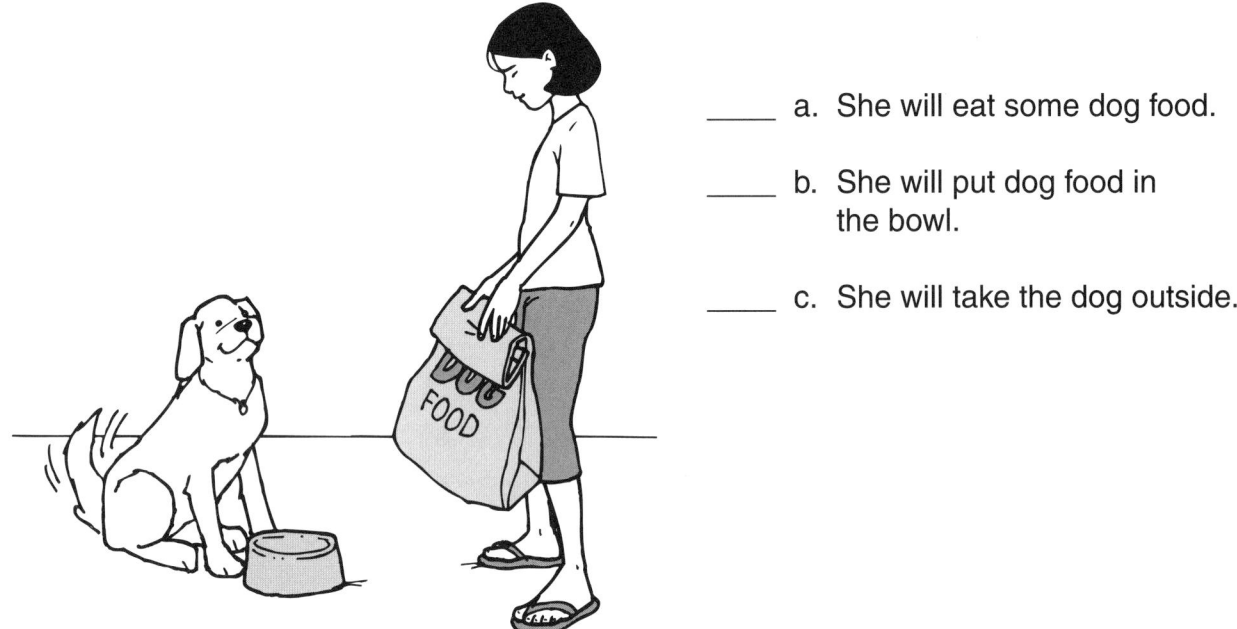

____ a. She will eat some dog food.

____ b. She will put dog food in the bowl.

____ c. She will take the dog outside.

2. This clown is at a birthday party. He just finished making another balloon animal. What will he do next?

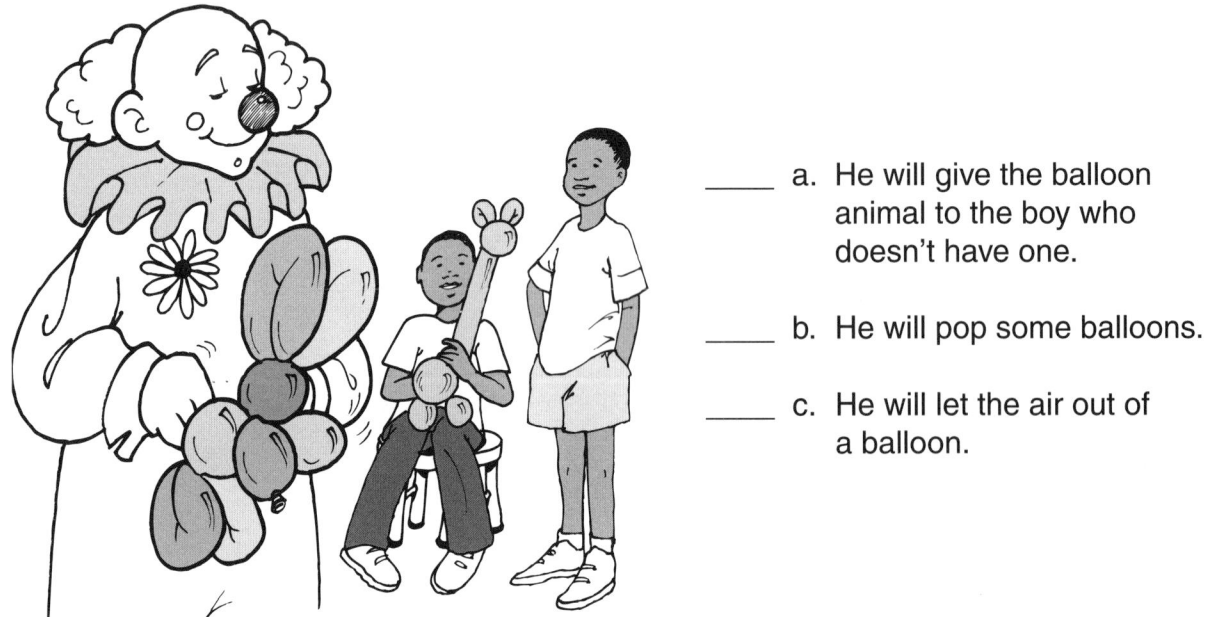

____ a. He will give the balloon animal to the boy who doesn't have one.

____ b. He will pop some balloons.

____ c. He will let the air out of a balloon.

Spotlight on Reasoning & Problem Solving
Making Predictions & Inferences

Predicting with Pictures ❷

➡ Look at each picture carefully. Then check the best answer to the question.

1. Clara just tipped over a bucket of sand. What will she do next?

____ a. She will sit on the bucket.

____ b. She will lift the bucket up carefully.

____ c. She will kick the bucket.

2. Evan tripped over a rock and fell down. What will he do next?

____ a. He will sing a song.

____ b. He will take a nap.

____ c. He will go take care of his knees.

Spotlight on Reasoning & Problem Solving
Making Predictions & Inferences

Predicting from Book Covers ❶

→ Look at each book cover. Then tell what the book might be about.

Predicting from Book Covers ❷

→ Look at each book cover. Then tell what the book might be about.

Predicting with Choices ❶

→ Check the best answer to each question.

1. What will happen to a flower if you pick it?

    ____ a. It will melt.

    ____ b. It will die.

    ____ c. It will grow new leaves.

2. What might happen if you skate on thin ice?

    ____ a. You might fall through the ice.

    ____ b. The ice might get colder.

    ____ c. The ice might get thicker.

3. What would happen if you put your finger in the flame of a candle?

    ____ a. You would burn the candle.

    ____ b. You would burn your finger.

    ____ c. The flame would get brighter.

4. What will happen if you mail a letter without a stamp on it?

    ____ a. The letter will stay in the mailbox.

    ____ b. The letter might get lost.

    ____ c. The person you sent the letter to will have to pay the postage.

Spotlight on Reasoning & Problem Solving
Making Predictions & Inferences

Predicting with Choices ❷

→ Check the best answer to each question.

1. What will happen if you leave a sandwich where a hungry dog could reach it?

    ____ a. The sandwich will poison the dog.

    ____ b. The dog will eat the sandwich.

    ____ c. The dog will ignore the sandwich.

2. If you put a sailboat and a rock into water, what will happen?

    ____ a. The boat will sink and the rock will float.

    ____ b. The boat and the rock will both float.

    ____ c. The boat will float and the rock will sink.

3. Brenda's ice-cream sundae was served without a spoon. What will Brenda do?

    ____ a. She will use her fingers to eat the sundae.

    ____ b. She will ask for a spoon to eat the sundae.

    ____ c. She will get a straw to eat the sundae.

4. Jeremy is making brownies for his family. He measured the water and put it into the bowl. What will he do next?

    ____ a. He will put the mix and the eggs into the bowl.

    ____ b. He will stir the water.

    ____ c. He will bake the brownies.

Predicting with Choices ❸

➜ Check the best answer to each question.

1. What will happen if you sit on a bag of potato chips?
   ____ a. The chips will taste saltier.
   ____ b. The chips will be crushed.
   ____ c. The bag will melt.

2. What will happen if you sit in a puddle of water?
   ____ a. The puddle will disappear.
   ____ b. Your pants will get wet.
   ____ c. Your arms will itch.

3. What will happen if you put ice into a glass of water?
   ____ a. The water will become cooler.
   ____ b. The water will freeze.
   ____ c. The glass will crack.

4. What will happen if someone throws a rock at a window?
   ____ a. The rock will break.
   ____ b. The glass in the window will crack or break.
   ____ c. The rock will bounce off the glass.

5. What will happen if you plant a seed and water it?
   ____ a. The seed will spoil.
   ____ b. The water will turn into a seed.
   ____ c. The seed will grow into a plant.

6. What will happen if you poke a balloon with a pin?
   ____ a. The pin will bend.
   ____ b. The balloon will get bigger.
   ____ c. The balloon will pop.

7. What will happen if you walk in rain without a raincoat or an umbrella?
   ____ a. Your clothes will stay dry.
   ____ b. Your clothes will get wet.
   ____ c. It will stop raining.

8. What might happen if you wear jeans that have a hole in a pocket?
   ____ a. Something might fall through the hole.
   ____ b. The whole might get smaller.
   ____ c. The pocket might fall off your jeans.

Spotlight on Reasoning & Problem Solving
Making Predictions & Inferences

Copyright © 2007 LinguiSystems, Inc.

Predicting with Choices ❹

→ Check the best answer to each question.

1. What will happen if you leave a glass of lemonade in a freezer?
   ____ a. The freezer will taste sour.
   ____ b. The lemonade will freeze.
   ____ c. The lemonade will get warm.

2. What will happen to white paint if you mix some red paint into it?
   ____ a. The paint will turn black.
   ____ b. The paint will stay white.
   ____ c. The paint will turn pink.

3. What will happen if you put a fresh stick of gum into your mouth?
   ____ a. The gum will turn soft as you chew it.
   ____ b. The gum will crack as you chew it.
   ____ c. The gum will make your teeth stick together.

4. What will happen if you turn a glass of milk upside down?
   ____ a. The glass will break.
   ____ b. The milk will spill out of the glass.
   ____ c. The milk will stay in the glass.

5. You are going to give someone a present. What will the person say to you?
   ____ a. Excuse me.
   ____ b. I'm sorry.
   ____ c. Thank you.

6. What will happen if you boil a raw potato?
   ____ a. It will explode.
   ____ b. It will turn softer as it cooks.
   ____ c. It will burn.

7. What will happen to bathwater if you unplug the drain?
   ____ a. More water will fill the tub.
   ____ b. The water will get soapy.
   ____ c. The water will drain out of the tub.

8. What will happen if you drop a stone into a pond?
   ____ a. The stone will sink.
   ____ b. The stone will float.
   ____ c. The stone will break.

Spotlight on Reasoning & Problem Solving
Making Predictions & Inferences

Predicting ❶

→ Write your answer for each question.

1. Your family planned a picnic for Saturday at the park. What will happen if it rains on Saturday?

   _____

2. You and your parent are shopping for groceries. You each want a different cereal. What will happen?

   _____

3. You just remembered that you haven't fed your goldfish for several days. What will happen?

   _____

4. Juan is feeding goats in a petting zoo. The goats have eaten all of the food Juan bought for them, and they are still hungry. What might happen?

   _____

5. You forgot to do your homework for today. What will happen?

   _____

6. Your teacher will be in meetings all day tomorrow. What will happen with your class?

   _____

7. The school nurse checked your eyes. She thinks you need glasses. What will happen?

   _____

Spotlight on Reasoning & Problem Solving
Making Predictions & Inferences

Predicting ❷

→ Write your answer for each question.

1. Your class is having an election. Everyone has put a vote in a box. What will happen next?

2. Clouds in the sky are getting dark and it's getting windy. What might happen?

3. The lights in the theater are being turned down. What will happen?

4. You are working on a computer when a thunderstorm begins. The computer screen flickers every few minutes. What might happen?

5. Your class is going on a field trip today. You forgot to bring in your signed permission slip. What might happen?

6. You slept late this morning and now you will be late for school. What will happen?

7. You planted some seeds in a pot and watered them. You set them on a windowsill where they will get some sun. You water them every other day. What will happen?

Spotlight on Reasoning & Problem Solving
Making Predictions & Inferences

Identifying Causes ❶

→ Look at each picture and think about what is happening. Then check the best answer to identify the reason or cause for each situation.

1. Tami's blow-dryer doesn't work. What is the reason her dryer doesn't work?

    ____ a. The motor is broken.

    ____ b. It isn't plugged in.

    ____ c. It is clogged with dust.

2. These students were working in their classroom. They heard a loud, ringing sound. What might have caused the sound and why?

    ____ a. The bell rang for the end of the school day.

    ____ b. An alarm went off because the classroom is too hot.

    ____ c. The alarm sounded because there is a fire drill.

3. Lisa is angry. Why is she angry?

    ____ a. She doesn't like being told to do the dishes.

    ____ b. She has too much homework.

    ____ c. She didn't get any dessert tonight.

Spotlight on Reasoning & Problem Solving
Making Predictions & Inferences

Identifying Causes ❷

→ Look at each picture and think about what is happening. Then check the best answer to identify the reason or cause for each situation.

1. These boys are on a canoe trip.
   Why are they carrying their canoe?

   ____ a. The water is too cold today.

   ____ b. They are using the canoe to get shade from the sun.

   ____ c. They are walking around some rapids in the river.

2. This man works in a bakery.
   Why is he wearing a hairnet?

   ____ a. He is having a bad hair day.

   ____ b. The net keeps his hair from getting into food.

   ____ c. He thinks it looks cool.

3. Kenya is putting money into her piggy bank.
   Why is she saving money?

   ____ a. Her parents make her save her money.

   ____ b. She wants to hide her money.

   ____ c. She wants to buy a bicycle.

Spotlight on Reasoning & Problem Solving
Making Predictions & Inferences

Identifying Causes ❸

→ Sometimes there can be more than one cause for an event. Check each possible reason for each situation.

1. Linda's mom is giving her some medicine. Why does Linda need medicine?

    ____ a. She has a cold.

    ____ b. She has the flu.

    ____ c. She didn't eat her breakfast.

2. Paul put two quarters in his pocket before he went to school. Now school is over and only one quarter is left in Paul's pocket. Why?

    ____ a. Someone gave him another quarter.

    ____ b. He used one quarter to pay for something.

    ____ c. One quarter dropped out of his pocket.

3. Matt spent the evening at a local carnival. He rode lots of rides and ate hot dogs, cotton candy, and a large milk shake. Now Matt doesn't feel well. What might be the cause?

    ____ a. He is hungry.

    ____ b. He ate too much junk food.

    ____ c. The rides made him dizzy.

4. After lunch, Maurice went to the office. He came back to class with an ice bag on his head. What might be the cause?

    ____ a. Maurice had a headache.

    ____ b. Maurice bought the ice pack from a vending machine.

    ____ c. Maurice had a bump on his head from an accident on the playground.

5. Melissa cleaned her hamster's cage and closed the door to the cage before she left the room. An hour later, the cage door was open and her hamster was gone. What might have caused this situation?

    ____ a. The door wasn't closed properly before.

    ____ b. The hamster asked someone to open the door.

    ____ c. Someone else let the hamster out of its cage.

Spotlight on Reasoning & Problem Solving
Making Predictions & Inferences

Identifying Causes ❹

➜ Sometimes there can be more than one cause for an event. Check each possible reason for each situation.

1. Jasmine broke her arm a few days ago. It doesn't hurt anymore. Her dad is drawing a picture on her cast. Why is he doing that?

    ____ a. He wants Jasmine to learn how to draw a clown.

    ____ b. He is decorating her cast for her.

    ____ c. He is trying to make her feel good.

2. Raymond was playing in the park this summer afternoon. Now he keeps scratching his arm. Why might his arm itch?

    ____ a. He got a mosquito bite.

    ____ b. He is having an allergic reaction to something he heard.

    ____ c. His arm is sunburned.

3. Jason carried a full bucket of water to the barn for the horses. When he got there, the bucket was only half full. What might have happened?

    ____ a. He drank some of the water.

    ____ b. Some of the water spilled out while he was walking.

    ____ c. There was a leak in the bucket.

4. Some birds built a nest in a nearby tree. Why is the nest empty now?

    ____ a. The birds are out looking for food.

    ____ b. The birds didn't like their nest.

    ____ c. The mother bird hasn't laid her eggs in the nest yet.

5. Yesterday this plant was healthy, but today it has wilted. What might have caused the plant to wilt?

    ____ a. It didn't get enough water.

    ____ b. It got too much water.

    ____ c. It got too hot or too much sunlight.

Spotlight on Reasoning & Problem Solving
Making Predictions & Inferences

Making Inferences with Pictures ❶

➡ Read these stories and answer the questions.

1. Molly and her dad went to the park and took their dog, Bingo. They found an open field and played ball with Bingo. Molly would throw the ball and Bingo would bring it back to her.

    a. Why did Molly and her dad look for an open field?

    _____

    b. How do you think Molly felt when Bingo brought the ball back to her?

    _____

    c. Why didn't Molly take Bingo to the park without her dad?

    _____

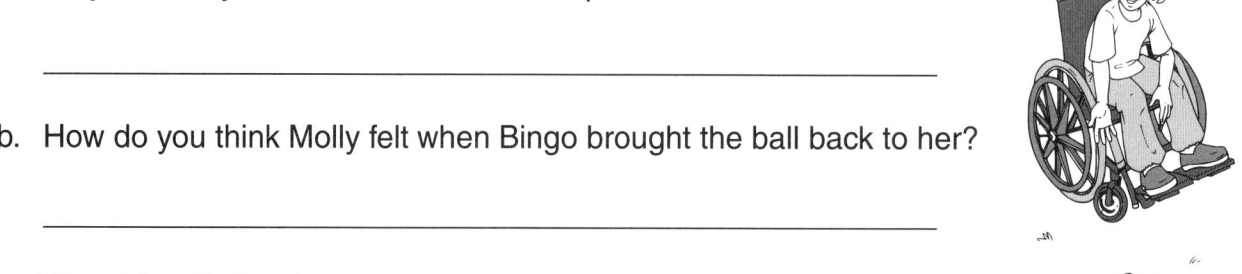

2. It has been a long day for the Garcia family. They began their trip at six in the morning. It is now 8:00 in the evening.

    a. Where are the Garcias now?
       Tell how you know.

    _____

    _____

    _____

    b. Why is the dad inspecting the suitcase?

    _____

    c. Why do you think the little girl is pulling on her mom's hand?

    _____

Spotlight on Reasoning & Problem Solving
Making Predictions & Inferences

Making Inferences with Pictures ❷

→ Read these stories and answer the questions.

1. At first, Erin could hardly see some of the small creatures. It was easier to see the larger ones. After a while, she spotted lots of small creatures both in the water and in the sand.

   a. Where was Erin? Tell why you think so.

   _____

   _____

   b. Why do you think an adult was with Erin?

   _____

   c. How do you know this scene is not in a classroom?

   _____

2. Every day at half past three, Mrs. Horner goes for a walk with Hugo. They usually walk about one mile. Then they go inside for a snack.

   a. Who is Hugo?

   _____

   _____

   b. Why does Hugo wear an unusual leash?

   _____

   c. Mrs. Horner is blind. How do you think she crosses streets safely?

   _____

Making Inferences with Pictures ❸

→ Read these stories and answer the questions.

1. Lily has been looking forward to this for months. Finally the day is here! She holds little John carefully. He is wrapped snuggly in a blanket from head to toe.

    a. Where is Lily sitting?

    _____

    _____

    b. Who is little John?

    _____

    _____

    c. Why is the woman in the bed smiling at Lily?

    _____

2. It is after dinner at Rosa's house.

    a. Where is Rosa?

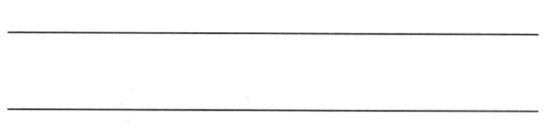

    _____

    _____

    b. Who is talking to Rosa?

    _____

    _____

    c. What do you think he is saying to Rosa?

    _____

Spotlight on Reasoning & Problem Solving
Making Predictions & Inferences

Making Inferences with Pictures ❹

→ Read these stories and answer the questions.

1. Jake and his dog, Ringo, went for a walk in the park this morning. There were still lots of puddles in the dog area from the rain last night. Jake let Ringo run around and Ringo got lots of exercise.

    a. What kind of weather is it today for Jake and Ringo?

    _____

    _____

    b. How does Jake feel about Ringo?

    _____

    _____

    c. Why is Jake filling a large tub with water?

    _____

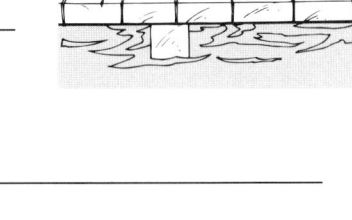

2. Dad tied Meg's straps and said, "Okay, we're all set. Follow me!"

    a. What are these children wearing? Why?

    _____

    _____

    b. Why isn't the dad wearing a life jacket?

    _____

    _____

Spotlight on Reasoning & Problem Solving
Making Predictions & Inferences

Making Inferences with Pictures 5

→ Read these stories and answer the questions.

1. Finally Jody is allowed to walk to school by herself.

    a. How does Jody feel?

    _____

    _____

    b. What is Jody doing now? Why?

    _____

    _____

2. Ron and Tasha have a babysitter tonight. Their bedtime is 8:00. It's 9:00 now.

    a. What are Ron and Tasha doing? Why?

    _____

    _____

    _____

    b. How does the babysitter feel? Why?

    _____

    _____

    _____

Spotlight on Reasoning & Problem Solving
Making Predictions & Inferences

Making Inferences Without Pictures ❶

→ Think about each situation and check the best answer(s) for the questions.

1. Before the soccer game today, Josh's uniform was spotless. After the game, his uniform had many grass stains and streaks of dirt.

   Which statement is true?
   ____ a. Josh didn't get to play in the game today.
   ____ b. Josh played in the game today.
   ____ c. Josh needs a new uniform.

2. Manuel and Devon are in the same class. Their parents bought the exact same school supplies for the boys just before school began this year. Manuel's supplies cost $15.95 but Devon's supplies cost $11.38.

   What could explain why the boys' supplies cost different amounts? Check each logical answer.
   ____ a. The parents bought the supplies at different stores.
   ____ b. Devon's parents bought the supplies on sale.
   ____ c. Devon's parents didn't buy all of the supplies.

3. "Maybe this time it won't hurt," Mandy told herself. She remembered the last time. Her jaw was sore for hours and her lips were so numb she couldn't even drink water without drooling. Last time, she had two fillings. This time, there would just be one. Mandy tried to play her small video game while she waited. Only one other patient was waiting in the room. Mandy hoped she would be called in next.

   Where was Mandy?
   ____ a. in a doctor's waiting room
   ____ b. in the school office
   ____ c. in a dentist's waiting room

   How did Mandy feel?
   ____ a. proud
   ____ b. nervous
   ____ c. lonely

4. Keshia could hardly wait to get home from school. Today might be the day! Her cat might already be a mother. "I'll bet she's waiting to show me her surprise," thought Keshia.

   What special thing did Keshia think happened while she was at school today?
   ____ a. Her cat had kittens.
   ____ b. Her dog had puppies.
   ____ c. Her cat learned a new trick.

Spotlight on Reasoning & Problem Solving
Making Predictions & Inferences

Making Inferences Without Pictures ❷

→ Think about each situation and check the best answer(s) for the questions.

1. Brian did his best to solve the math problems on the test. Then he looked them over carefully. "Oops, that answer is wrong," he thought. He drew a neat line through the wrong answer and wrote the correct answer beside it.

   Why didn't Brian just erase the wrong answer? Check each logical reason.
   _____ a. It would take too long to erase it.
   _____ b. His teacher didn't allow erasing on a math test.
   _____ c. He had done his work in ink.

2. Diego enjoyed talking with Mr. Hooper, an elderly neighbor. Today Diego noticed something odd about Mr. Hooper's house. There were several newspapers on the front stoop. The yard hadn't been mowed and the grass was long. There were a few palm leaves lying around the yard.

   What might have happened?
   _____ a. Mr. Hooper might be sick.
   _____ b. Mr. Hooper might not care if his yard looked neat.
   _____ c. Mr. Hooper might be on a trip.
   _____ d. Mr. Hooper might be in a hospital.

3. Tyler was careful not to step on any broken pieces. He got the dustpan and brush and cleaned the mess on the floor. "Oh, well," he thought, "at least I hadn't already poured my juice."

   What had happened?
   _____ a. Tyler dropped a bowl on the floor and it broke.
   _____ b. Tyler dropped a plate on the floor and it shattered.
   _____ c. Tyler dropped a glass on the floor and it broke.

4. Jeff's mom wasn't home when he walked in the door after school, but he wasn't worried. He knew she would be home in a few minutes.

   Why was Jeff so sure his mom would be home soon? Check each logical answer.
   _____ a. She had told him when she would get home.
   _____ b. She always came home at the same time every day.
   _____ c. He hoped she would come home soon.
   _____ d. His mom left him a note saying when she would get home.

Spotlight on Reasoning & Problem Solving
Making Predictions & Inferences

Making Inferences Without Pictures ❸

→ Think about each situation and check the best answer(s) for the questions.

1. Terry and his friends usually get together at the park to play basketball every Saturday morning. Today everyone got there on time, but they couldn't play.

   Why couldn't they play? Check each logical reason.
   ____ a. Someone else was already using the court.
   ____ b. They were arguing with each other.
   ____ c. No one had brought a basketball.
   ____ d. The only basketball was flat.
   ____ e. It was Saturday.

2. Diana and Cody couldn't believe their eyes. By the end of the day, all that was left in the yard was an old hat, a long carrot, and some rocks. Grass poked up through the few patches of snow.

   What had been in the yard earlier in the day?
   ____ a. a wheelbarrow with tools
   ____ b. a scarecrow
   ____ c. a snowman

3. Mike wanted to become invisible. Why did he have to be in this piano recital anyway? Bravely, he took his place at the piano when it was his turn to play. "I hope all those hours pay off," he thought.

   What did Mike mean about all the hours paying off?
   ____ a. His piano recital was expensive.
   ____ b. He had practiced for hours.
   ____ c. He wished he had practiced more.

4. Tracy sat quietly beside her packed suitcase. She was wearing her new jacket and she was holding her new camera. She couldn't wait to snap some great shots of the trip. Her dad came back from getting gas and said, "Wow, I guess you're all ready to go!"

   How did Tracy's dad know she was ready to go?
   ____ a. She told him she was ready.
   ____ b. Her suitcase was packed and she had her jacket on.
   ____ c. He asked her if she was ready yet.

Spotlight on Reasoning & Problem Solving
Making Predictions & Inferences

Making Inferences Without Pictures ❹

→ Think about each situation and check the best answer(s) for the questions.

1. Rhonda went to the library and got some books for her report. She could open the library door with no problem, but she couldn't open the door to her house.

   Why couldn't Rhonda open the door to her house? Check each logical answer.
   ____ a. The door was already open.
   ____ b. She didn't have a key to unlock the door.
   ____ c. Her arms were too tired.
   ____ d. She needed her arms and hands to hold onto the books.

2. Abby was having dinner at her friend Deena's home tonight. As everyone passed the food around, Abby helped herself to chicken and carrots and salad, but she didn't take any mashed potatoes.

   Why didn't Abby take any mashed potatoes? Check each logical answer.
   ____ a. She didn't care for mashed potatoes.
   ____ b. She is allergic to dairy products.
   ____ c. She is trying to lose weight.
   ____ d. She doesn't eat vegetables.

3. Jim woke up and rubbed his eyes. He looked at the clock and thought, "That can't be right! I know it's not 2:00 in the morning."

   How did Jim know his clock didn't show the correct time?
   ____ a. It was too dark outside to be 2:00 in the morning.
   ____ b. It was too light outside to be 2:00 in the morning.
   ____ c. It was an old clock.

   What could explain why the clock showed the wrong time? Check each logical answer.
   ____ a. The clock needed new batteries.
   ____ b. It was the wrong clock.
   ____ c. The power had gone off earlier.
   ____ d. Someone had changed the time setting on the clock.

4. Noah usually left for school by 7:30, but it is already 9:00 today and Noah is still home.

   Why might Noah still be home? Check each logical answer.
   ____ a. It is a holiday today.
   ____ b. Noah is playing a joke on his family.
   ____ c. Noah is sick.
   ____ d. It is Sunday.

Spotlight on Reasoning & Problem Solving
Making Predictions & Inferences

Making Inferences Without Pictures ❺

→ Think about each situation and check the best answer(s) for the questions.

1. Mrs. Lee loaded her groceries into her trunk and took the cart to the storage area. As she approached her car, she put her hands up to her face and cried, "Oh, no!"

   How did Mrs. Lee feel?
   ____ a. thrilled
   ____ b. upset
   ____ c. guilty

   What might be the reason Mrs. Lee said, "Oh, no!"? Check each logical answer.
   ____ a. She couldn't remember where her car was.
   ____ b. There were dents or scratches on her car.
   ____ c. Something was leaking from her car.
   ____ d. Her car had been painted a different color.

2. Tara spent hours on the phone or online with her boyfriend. Tonight she got a call from him right after dinner. After a few minutes, Tara burst into tears, slammed the phone down, and closed herself up in her bedroom.

   What might be the reason Tara acted this way? Check each logical answer.
   ____ a. Tara and her boyfriend broke up.
   ____ b. Tara and her boyfriend had an argument.
   ____ c. Tara realized she needed to do her homework.

3. Mr. Garcia and his family drove past North Stadium after dinner. There was heavy traffic and the stadium lights were on. "There must be a game tonight," said Mr. Garcia.

   What made Mr. Garcia think there was a game tonight? Check each logical answer.
   ____ a. They were driving past the stadium.
   ____ b. There was a lot of traffic.
   ____ c. Lights were on in the stadium.

4. The school nurse said, "Zack, this time please cover your left eye and read the smallest letters you can see on the chart." Zack read the letters and then the next student took his place.

   What was going on?
   ____ a. The school nurse was testing students' hearing.
   ____ b. Zack was taking a reading test.
   ____ c. Students were getting their eyes tested by the school nurse.

Spotlight on Reasoning & Problem Solving
Making Predictions & Inferences

Answer Key

Pretest/Posttest
1. Orange juice isn't hot.
2. You can't see your shadow when it's rainy/cloudy.
3. She got a bad grade/score.
4. Answers will vary.
5. He didn't close the drain.
6. The table hadn't been cleaned yet.
7. Upset, because Dan had broken his promise to keep Kelly's secret
8. Answers will vary.
9. Answers will vary.
10. Answers will vary.

page 10
1. The boy is jumping rope in the rain.
2. Some of the items the man is juggling are silly.
3. Turtles can't blow bubbles.
4. You can't walk a fish.

page 11
1. You wouldn't use a machine to make a peanut butter and jelly sandwich.
2. sock nailed on roof, car parked sideways, birthday cake on top of car, dog sitting on car, snake and frog on roof, bear watching from behind a bush

page 12
1. b
2. a
3. b
4. a

page 13
1. b
2. c

page 14
1. c
2. b

page 15
1. shoelaces
2. eye
3. sleeve
4. leg
5. tires
6. mouth

page 16
1. b
2. a

page 17
1. b
2. c

pages 18-19
Answers will vary.

page 20
1. b
2. a
3. b
4. c

page 21
1. b
2. c
3. b
4. a

page 22
1. b
2. b
3. a
4. b
5. c
6. c
7. b
8. a

page 23
1. b
2. c
3. a
4. b
5. c
6. b
7. c
8. a

pages 24-25
Answers will vary.

page 26
1. b
2. c
3. a

page 27
1. c
2. b
3. c

page 28
1. a, b
2. b, c
3. b, c
4. a, c
5. a, c

page 29
1. b, c
2. a, c
3. b, c
4. a, c
5. a, c

pages 30-34
Answers will vary.

page 35
1. b
2. a, b
3. c; b
4. a

page 36
1. b, c
2. a, c, d
3. c
4. a, b, d

page 37
1. a, c, d
2. c
3. b
4. b

page 38
1. b, d
2. a, b, c
3. b; a, c, d
4. a, c, d

page 39
1. b; b, c
2. a, b
3. b, c
4. c